UNDER THE MOON

The sun is a huge, burning ball of fire. On the planet Earth we cannot live without heat and light from the sun. Around our planet, there is the ozone layer, which protects us from the sun's fire. But what happens if the ozone layer breaks up? Today there are already small holes in it, and some people say they will get bigger and bigger – until one day there will be nothing between us and the sun's fire.

It happened in 2222. So the people of Earth made the AOL – the Artificial Ozone Layer. Another thousand years of life for the beautiful planet Earth. Trees grew again, rain fell, there was water in the rivers . . .

But now it is 2522, and the AOL is already breaking up. The new forests are beginning to burn, the rivers are running dry. Kiah and Rilla, from their spaceship, see the danger, but what can they do? Their friends in the colony under the moon are a long way away, and Gog, the Earth Commander, will not listen to them.

OXFORD BOOKWORMS LIBRARY
Fantasy & Horror

Under the Moon
Stage 1 (400 headwords)

Series Editor: Jennifer Bassett
Founder Editor: Tricia Hedge
Activities Editors: Jennifer Bassett and Alison Baxter

الحمد رب العالمين

ROWENA AKINYEMI

Under the Moon

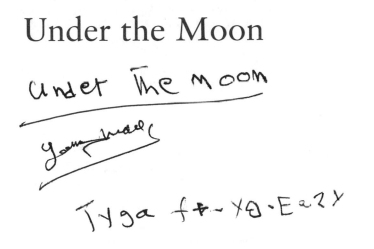

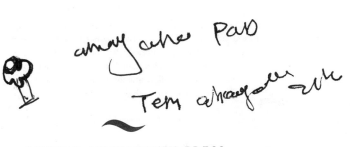

OXFORD UNIVERSITY PRESS

Oxford University Press
Great Clarendon Street, Oxford OX2 6DP

Oxford   New York
Athens Auckland Bangkok Bogotá Buenos Aires Cape Town
Chennai Dar es Salaam Delhi Florence Hong Kong Istanbul Karachi Kolkata
Kuala Lumpur Madrid Melbourne Mexico City Mumbai Nairobi
Paris São Paulo Shanghai Singapore Taipei Tokyo Toronto Warsaw
with associated companies in
Berlin Ibadan

OXFORD and OXFORD ENGLISH
are trade marks of Oxford University Press

ISBN 0 19 422955 6

© Oxford University Press 2000

Third impression 2001

First published in Oxford Bookworms 1992
This second edition published in the Oxford Bookworms Library 2000

Illustrated by Peter Richardson

Printed in Spain by Unigraf s.l.

CONTENTS

Back   Forward   Reload   Home   Search   Guide   Images

Universal Planet News   01.01.2222

ALWAYS REMEMBER TODAY! A WONDERFUL DAY FOR THE PLANET EARTH!

THE ARTIFICIAL OZONE LAYER (AOL) IS FINISHED!

Today the last Ship arrived from space at 1500 hours. In Kisangani, fifty thousand people waited for Ship OL–20, the last of the AOL Ships.

Ship OM–1 is staying in space with its satellite. They are watching the AOL, day and night.

Now Earth can begin to live again! Under the AOL the sun cannot burn us. Trees and people can now have water again and stay alive. The AOL is good for a thousand years!

UNIVERSAL PLANET NEWS: IT'S OUT OF THIS WORLD!

1

The AOL in 2522

Five hundred kilometres over Europe, Ship OM–45 moved north. In a room at the back of the ship, Kiah watched the numbers on the computer in front of him.

'Time for dinner,' Rilla said.

Kiah watched the numbers on the computer.

The numbers changed quickly and Kiah's eyes didn't move. Rilla went across the room to his table. She began to watch the numbers, too.

'What's wrong with the satellite?' she asked. She was a beautiful girl, about twenty years old, with long black hair and big eyes.

'Nothing's wrong with the satellite,' Kiah answered quietly. 'It's the AOL.' He began to write the numbers in the book on his table.

Suddenly, the numbers stopped changing. Kiah looked at Rilla. 'Over Europe,' he said. 'It's happening. The AOL is breaking up. There are big holes in the AOL and they're getting bigger.'

'You're right! Shall we see Captain Seru now, before dinner?'

Kiah stood up. He was nearly two metres tall, with dark eyes and hair. 'Yes, come on,' he said.

Quickly, they went to Captain Seru's room. They waited at the door.

'Come in!' Captain Seru called. She was a little woman with a fat face. 'Come in! Would you like a drink?'

'No, thank you,' Kiah answered. 'I'd like you to look at these numbers.' Kiah gave Captain Seru his book.

Captain Seru looked at the numbers. Suddenly, her face changed. 'No, no,' she said. 'I don't want to talk. It's late and I'm tired. Sit down and have a drink.'

3

Kiah and Rilla sat down. There was a big window in Captain Seru's room. Kiah looked out of the window at the dark sky. He saw the Moon. It was cold and white in the dark sky.

'Captain Seru,' he began. 'It's important. Look at those numbers carefully. The AOL is beginning to—'

'Stop!' Captain Seru stood up and put her hands in her pockets. She went to the window and looked at the sky.

'Three hundred years ago, Earth nearly died,' Rilla said. 'Earth stopped dying because of the AOL. But now, over Europe, the AOL is breaking up. We would like you to talk to Earth Commander.'

Captain Seru did not move. 'Do you remember Adai?' she asked. She didn't wait for an answer. 'I was on his ship, two years ago. One evening, the satellite gave us interesting numbers about the AOL. We went back to Earth and saw Earth Commander.' Captain Seru stopped speaking.

Rilla looked at Kiah. 'And then?' she asked Captain Seru.

'Gog was angry, very angry,' Captain Seru said. 'In the end, he sent Adai to the Moon. Adai's there now, Commander of the Moon colony, under the Moon.'

Kiah waited for a second or two. 'I know about Adai. But we need to talk to Earth Commander again. These numbers are worse.'

'Do you remember Adai?' Captain Seru asked.

Captain Seru's face went red. 'You don't understand. I'm not going to talk to Gog. Last time, he sent me to a weather ship in the Antarctic! This is my first Ship for two years!' And Captain Seru began drinking.

Kiah stood up. 'Thank you, Captain Seru.'

Captain Seru said nothing.

Kiah and Rilla left the room, and walked slowly downstairs. The Ship was dark and quiet. It was eight o'clock and everybody was at dinner.

'What are we going to do next?' Rilla asked.

'I need to talk to Adai,' Kiah said.

'OK, talk to Adai. But he's far away on the Moon colony,' Rilla said. 'Let's visit Commander Zadak.'

'Zadak? Commander of Australia? He's famous!'

'Yes. He's my father's friend. He worked with my father in Brazil ten years ago. Perhaps he can help us.'

Kiah smiled. 'Good! We return to Earth next week. I can phone Adai from Kisangani and then we can go to Australia. But now, I'm hungry! Let's get some dinner.'

2

Visit to Australia

On Friday, after three weeks in space, Kiah and Rilla finished work and left Ship OM–45 on a space plane to

Kiah and Rilla took a space plane to Kisangani.

Kisangani. Kiah phoned Adai and Rilla phoned Commander Zadak in Australia. The next morning they took an aeroplane to Sydney. A taxi took them from the airport to Commander Zadak's office, some kilometres north of Sydney.

'Wait for us here,' Kiah said to the taxi driver.

Kiah and Rilla walked to the gate. About ten guards stood in front of the gate. Across the road, a train waited.

'Rilla, OM–45,' Rilla said. 'To see Commander Zadak at four-thirty.'

'Let me call the Commander's office,' the guard said.

Kiah and Rilla waited. It was hot and Kiah began to feel thirsty.

The guard came back. 'I'm sorry,' he said. 'The Commander can't see you.'

'But I talked to the Commander yesterday,' Rilla said. 'He wanted to see us at four-thirty.'

'The Commander is leaving on the train in three minutes,' the guard said.

'Can we wait and see him here?' Kiah asked.

'No!' the guard shouted. 'Get out of here!'

Kiah and Rilla walked back to the taxi.

'Where's the driver?' Kiah asked.

'Look! He's sitting by that wall,' Rilla said.

Just then, Commander Zadak came out of the gate. He was a very tall, big man with blue eyes and a lot of white hair. Two guards marched in front of him, and two guards marched behind him. They all carried guns.

'There he is!' Rilla cried. 'Commander!' And she began to run along the road to him.

Commander Zadak did not stop. A guard opened the door of the train and the Commander got in. Slowly, the train began to move.

Kiah ran to the taxi and jumped in. Then he drove the taxi fast down the road. The taxi driver saw him and ran after him. The train began to move faster. Suddenly, Kiah drove the taxi off the road. He drove in front of the train and stopped.

The train came nearer. And then the train stopped,

The train stopped, and some guards jumped off.

very near the taxi, and some guards jumped off. Kiah opened the door and got out of the taxi.

'Put up your hands!' the guards shouted.

Two of the guards began to hit Kiah.

'Stop that!' someone shouted. 'Bring him over here!' It was Commander Zadak.

Kiah stood in front of the Commander. Just then, Rilla arrived.

'Oh, it's you!' Commander Zadak said. He did not smile. 'Rilla, your father's going to be angry.'

'We want to talk to you, Commander,' Rilla said. 'It's very important.'

'Very well. I'm listening.'

Kiah began to talk. 'Two years ago, Adai told you about the holes in the AOL. Now they're worse. The AOL is breaking up over Europe. Please look at these numbers and this satellite picture.'

He gave his book to Commander Zadak and the Commander looked at the numbers.

'It's important, Commander,' Kiah said. 'In ten years Earth is going to die.'

'You stopped my train because of this?' Commander Zadak asked. 'Two years ago Adai talked to me about the AOL. Then he talked to Earth Commander, and what happened? Where is Adai now? Is the Moon colony helping the AOL?'

'We know about Adai, Commander,' Rilla said. 'But someone needs to talk to Earth Commander again.'

'I'm going to talk to Gog about rain, I can tell you that. Earth needs rain: there was no rain last winter. Half of Australia has no water and my trees here are dying. Without rain, many people are going to die. Is Gog going to understand that? I don't know!'

Commander Zadak began to walk back to his train. 'Move that taxi!' he called to his guards.

Some guards moved the taxi back to the road and then they jumped on to the train again. The train began to move.

'OK,' the taxi driver shouted. 'What are you going to do next? Drive my taxi into the river?'

Kiah smiled. He took some money from his pocket and gave it to the taxi driver.

The taxi driver looked at the money. 'OK, OK,' he said. 'Where now? Back to the airport?'

Kiah took Rilla's hand. 'Yes,' he said. 'Let's get back to Kisangani. We can phone Adai again tomorrow.'

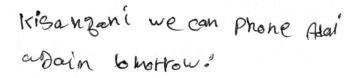

Back   Forward   Reload   Home   Search   Guide   Images

Universal Planet News   *12.06.2522*

MOON COMMANDER NEEDS MORE MONEY
RIVER NOW FINISHED

Commander Adai, from his space colony under the Moon, tells Earth: *We finished making the river last month – and it's beautiful! But we need more money.* Commander Adai and his people are working on the buildings now, and the buildings are nearly finished. But the roads are not ready. *We would like many people to live here soon,* the Commander told us on the phone. *But we need a lot of money!*

MOON COLONY

UNIVERSAL PLANET NEWS: IT'S OUT OF THIS WORLD!

3

Earth Commander

The next day in Kisangani, Kiah and Rilla waited quietly in an office in Gog's house. Suddenly, Commander Zadak came into the office and gave some letters to the man behind the table. He saw the two young people and stopped in front of them.

'You again!' he said. 'What are you doing here?'

Kiah stood up. 'Good morning, Commander. We're here because we want to see Earth Commander.'

'I saw Earth Commander some minutes ago and talked to him about rain,' Zadak said quietly. 'But he didn't listen. Your captain, Seru, was here earlier this morning and began to tell him about the holes in the AOL. But Gog doesn't want to hear about our planet. He's always talking about Mars. In the end, he's going to destroy Earth.'

'Please help us!' Rilla cried. 'Come and see Gog with us!'

'No.' Zadak looked at Kiah and then at Rilla with his blue eyes. 'I'm not talking to Gog again. And you – Gog isn't going to listen to you. Be careful – and good luck!'

Commander Zadak opened the door and left the office.

Rilla looked at Kiah. 'Earth Commander is a difficult man. I don't understand him.'

'Everyone is afraid of him,' Kiah said. 'And Commander Zadak isn't going to help us.'

Kiah and Rilla waited. They waited and waited. At nearly twelve o'clock, a guard came into the office.

'Come!' he said.

Kiah and Rilla went with the guard. The house was big and old, with big windows and many doors. The guard went downstairs and opened one of the doors. There was nobody in the room.

'Wait here,' the guard said, and left.

Kiah and Rilla sat down on the expensive green and black chairs and looked at the expensive flowers on the tables. There were no windows in this room. Suddenly, the door opened and a tall, fat woman came in. Her name was Bel, and she was Gog's wife. She had a lot of long red hair and she wore an expensive blue dress. Bel liked expensive things. She carried a cat. The cat was black and white: half its face was black and half was white; half its body was black and half was white.

'Why are you here? Why do you want to see Earth Commander?' she asked.

Rilla stood up. 'How do you do?' she said. 'We want to talk to Earth Commander about the AOL. We have new numbers from the satellite.'

'Why are you here?' Bel asked.

Bel's face was red. 'The AOL! Earth Commander knows about the AOL, and he is the best man—'

'Excuse me,' Kiah said quietly. 'We want to help Earth Commander.'

Bel began to laugh. 'Help? You?' The cat jumped down and walked across the room. 'How can you help? Why can't you understand? Listen. Earth Commander is working on the spaceship for Mars. It's difficult and expensive work.' The cat jumped on to Rilla's chair and looked at her with its yellow eyes. 'Two years ago, Adai wanted more money for the AOL – and Earth Commander sent him to the colony under the Moon. Now you're talking about the AOL. Do you want to go to the Moon, too?'

The door opened again and a different guard came in. 'Excuse me. Earth Commander is ready now.'

Bel stood up. 'You can see Earth Commander now,' she said coldly. 'But you're going to be sorry!'

The guard opened a different door, and Bel and the cat went into a beautiful room with expensive, very old tables and chairs. Rilla and Kiah went in behind them. There were no windows in the room, but a lot of pictures. There was Gog! The richest man on Earth; and the worst man on Earth. He was tall and fat, and without much hair. He sat behind a big table with a television, three computers and five telephones. He watched the television and didn't look at Kiah or Rilla. Two guards with guns stood behind him and two

Gog – the richest man on Earth.

more guards stood near the door.

'Here they are!' Bel said. 'They aren't friends, oh no! They want to talk about the AOL, of course. No one understands about Mars—'

'That's all right, that's all right,' Gog said quickly. And then he looked up, first at Rilla and then at Kiah. His eyes were cold and green. 'I know about you two,' he said. 'Your captain told me about you. You're famous! Two children! You want to help planet Earth, is that right?' He waited. The cat jumped on to his table and sat down in front of the television.

'Yes, Commander,' Kiah began. 'The AOL is breaking up—'

'When? Tonight? Tomorrow?' Gog said angrily. 'I heard this old story two years ago, from Adai. Everyone comes here and wants money – money for the AOL, money for rain, money for the Moon colony. But I am Earth Commander, and you are nobody! I know about the AOL and the AOL is good for a hundred years!'

'But the satellite—' Kiah began again.

'Be quiet!' Gog cried. 'I am Earth Commander! I'm not going to give money for the AOL! Or for rain! Or for the Moon!' Gog looked at the guards near the door. 'Take them – take them away. I don't want to hear them.'

The guards moved behind Kiah and Rilla, and Bel began to laugh. 'Goodbye!' she said. 'You're not going to the Moon, you're going to prison! You can talk about the holes in the AOL there!'

Universal Planet News 13.06.2522

NO RAIN! FORESTS ARE DYING!

The new forests in Europe, Asia and Africa are dying because there is no rain. The Commanders of Europe, Asia, America, Africa and Australia finished making the new forests ten years ago. The forests were very expensive. Commander Zadak, of Australia, was in Kisangani today. He talked to Earth Commander about rain. *My trees are dying,* he told us. *The forests are important to all of us. Without water nothing can live. Many hundreds of years ago the old forests died. Now it is happening again. After the forests die, then people are going to die, too.*

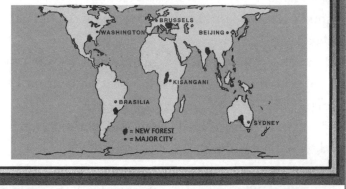

UNIVERSAL PLANET NEWS: IT'S OUT OF THIS WORLD!

4

Prison 888

Commander Zadak was in his room at the biggest hotel in Kisangani. Suddenly, he heard the phone.

'Commander?' someone said, very quietly. 'A man and a woman – from Ship OM–45 – in prison 888.' The phone went dead. Zadak put the phone down, stood up, and left his room.

Prison 888 was a big building without windows, near Gog's house. There were a lot of guards at the gate, and some more guards marched past the building. All the guards carried guns.

Commander Zadak walked across the road to the prison. 'I want to visit someone. My name is Commander Zadak.'

'I'm sorry, Commander,' a guard said. 'We can't open the gate. Nobody can go in without a letter from Earth Commander.'

'That's all right,' Zadak said, and walked along the road, past the prison.

A guard ran behind him. 'Excuse me, Commander,' he said quickly. 'Please come back tonight. I can open the back gate at midnight. You can see the two people from Ship OM–45.'

Prison 888 was a big building near Gog's house.

Zadak looked at the guard. 'Your captain's going to kill you.'

The guard smiled. 'My captain phoned you about the two people from OM–45. He's the brother of Captain Seru.'

Zadak didn't smile. 'The prison commander is going to kill you and your captain.'

'It doesn't matter,' the guard said. 'We want to help.'

'Midnight,' Zadak said, and walked away.

At midnight there were four guards at the front gate of prison 888, and there was one guard at the back gate. The guard opened the gate and Zadak went in. The guard said nothing. They walked downstairs into a big room. A lot of prisoners slept on the floor because there were no beds or chairs. Kiah and Rilla sat on the floor near the door.

'You can talk for five minutes,' the guard said quietly. 'The next guard arrives at 12.15.'

Kiah and Rilla stood up. 'Good evening, Commander,' they said.

Zadak looked at the prisoners. 'Why are all these people here?' he said to Kiah and Rilla. 'They're in prison because Gog doesn't like them. I talk to Gog about rain, I talk to him about the AOL, but he never listens. Today, someone told me about some fires in the new forest here in Africa; but Gog doesn't want to hear about those fires.' Zadak laughed angrily. 'And he doesn't want to hear

'Gog *never listens,' Zadak said angrily.*

about my trees in Australia. He never listens to me. He's always thinking about Mars, not about our beautiful planet Earth.'

Kiah listened carefully. 'Take it easy, Commander,' he said quietly. 'Please talk to Adai. Adai wants to help. He can come back from the Moon and help you.'

'No,' Zadak said. 'I phoned Adai this afternoon. He's a

23

good man and he wants to help. But I don't need help. I'm going to stop Gog – I'm going to kill him.'

Kiah closed his eyes for a minute. 'Gog's guards have guns. They can kill you, Commander,' he said. 'You need more people to help. Wait for Adai. He can help you to look for more people.'

'No, Kiah,' Zadak said quietly. 'I don't want more people. Adai can come back to Earth after Gog is dead – after I am dead, perhaps. I don't want Adai to die, too.'

'Excuse me, Commander,' the guard said. He looked at the clock near the door.

'OK. Let's go,' Zadak said to the guard. He looked at Rilla and then at Kiah. His eyes were very blue. 'Goodbye,' he said.

'Goodbye, Commander,' Kiah said.

'Be careful!' Rilla cried. 'And good luck!'

Early that morning, Earth Commander's house was quiet. A guard opened the door.

'Good morning, Commander Zadak,' he said. 'Earth Commander isn't in his office.'

'That's all right,' Zadak said. 'I can wait.'

Zadak went upstairs and waited.

At eight o'clock Bel came into the room. 'Good morning, Commander,' she said. 'You're early this morning. Are you happier today? Earth Commander was

For a second nobody moved.

very angry with you yesterday. Don't begin talking about rain or the AOL today.'

Zadak smiled, but his blue eyes were cold. 'No,' he said. 'I'm not going to talk about rain today.'

Just then, Gog came into the room. He looked at Zadak. 'What's wrong? Why are you here at eight o'clock in the morning?'

Zadak took his gun from his pocket. Gog saw the gun and his face went white. His eyes were dark and afraid. For a second nobody moved.

Suddenly, Bel's black and white cat ran into the room. 'Guards! Guards!' Bel shouted.

The cat jumped at Zadak, and Zadak hit the cat away from him. Bel ran across the room to Gog, and Zadak, at that second, shot at Gog. But Bel was between him and Gog. She gave a cry and fell to the floor. Her hair looked very red on the black floor.

'No!' Gog cried. 'You shot Bel!'

Three guards ran into the room with their big guns and stood in front of Gog.

'Kill him!' Gog shouted, and began to help Bel.

Zadak looked at the guards and then at Bel and Gog. Kiah was right: he was going to die.

'I'm sorry, Kiah. I'm sorry, Adai,' he said quietly.

The guards shot Zadak. Slowly, he fell to the floor.

WE CAN LIVE ON MARS!

Two spaceships – MARS 4 and 5 – are going to visit Mars this week. Two years ago, Ship MARS 1 visited Mars and began to change the planet. MARS 2 and 3 visited Mars last year and began to build the first town there. The planet is much warmer now, and three months ago, it began to rain on Mars. *We can live on planet Mars,* Earth Commander said today. *One day, soon, people are going to live on Mars and they are not going to come back to Earth.*

MARS
Day : 24.6 hours
Year : 687 days
−50° centigrade

6787 km

Town

Sun   Jupiter   Uranus   Pluto

Venus   Saturn

Mercury   Earth   Neptune
⤻ Mars
78300000 km

UNIVERSAL PLANET NEWS: IT'S OUT OF THIS WORLD!

27

5

Forest fires

Later that morning, four guards took Rilla to Gog's office. His face looked tired and his eyes were red.

Four guards took Rilla to Gog's office.

'Leave us,' he said to the guards. Then he looked at Rilla. 'Tell me about Kiah. When did you first meet him? Is Zadak his friend? What do they talk about?'

Rilla looked down at the floor and said nothing.

'Come on, tell me!' Gog said angrily. He waited, but Rilla said nothing. 'Tell me about Zadak, then. Your father and Commander Zadak were friends. Now, you're talking to Zadak about the AOL. I know that. What is Zadak saying?'

'Why? Why do you want to know about Commander Zadak?' Rilla asked.

'I'm asking the questions, not you,' Gog said. 'Did you see Zadak yesterday?'

'The AOL is important, not Commander Zadak,' Rilla said.

Gog watched Rilla carefully. 'Zadak is dead.'

'No!' Rilla cried.

'He is dead,' Gog said again. 'You lost your friend, here in this building, early this morning. My guards shot him.'

Rilla's face went white. 'What happened? Tell me!'

'I'm going to tell you one thing,' Gog said angrily. 'I'm going to destroy Australia. I'm going to burn Zadak's new forest there. You can tell all your friends! Zadak wanted to kill me, but I killed him. He wanted money for rain, money for the AOL, and now he's dead. You can tell all those prisoners in prison 888. They wanted to stop me, but they can't now. I'm going to Mars! Bel always wanted to go to Mars.' He began to hit the table with his hand. 'I'm going to leave this dead planet! Nobody can stop me!'

'You're crazy,' Rilla said. 'You killed Zadak, but one day someone is going to kill you.'

Gog stood up. His face was tired and he looked ill. 'Be quiet!' he said. 'Guards! Take her away. Back to 888.'

The guards came in and took Rilla out.

'What happened?' she asked them. 'Commander Zadak is dead. Why is Gog angry?'

The guards said nothing. But after they returned to the gate of 888, a guard said to Rilla, very quietly: 'Bel is dead. Zadak didn't shoot Gog, but he shot Bel, before the guards shot him.'

A guard took Rilla into the prison, and soon she was with Kiah again.

'What happened?' Kiah asked. 'Tell me.'

Rilla put her hands over her face and began to cry. 'Zadak is dead,' she began. 'He didn't kill Gog. He killed Bel before the guards shot him, and now Gog is going to destroy Australia.'

Kiah sat down on the floor next to Rilla. His face was sad. 'Don't cry,' he said quietly.

Three or four prisoners came across the room.

'What's the matter?' they asked.

'Zadak is dead,' Kiah said. 'But Bel is dead, too.'

'What's going to happen next?' someone asked. But nobody answered.

The next afternoon, Captain Seru's brother took Kiah and Rilla to a little room at the back of the prison. They sat down, and five minutes later Captain Seru arrived. Nobody smiled.

'You were right, Captain,' Kiah said. 'Gog sent us to prison because we told him about the holes in the AOL.'

Seru smiled. 'You were right, Kiah,' she said. 'Those satellite numbers were very bad. I began to tell Gog, but he didn't listen to me.'

'Would you like some coffee? And some sandwiches?' Seru's brother asked.

'Yes, please,' Seru said. 'I'm hungry.' She looked at Kiah and Rilla. 'Things are very bad.'

'What's happening?' Rilla asked.

'You know about Zadak? And Bel?'

'Yes. Gog told Rilla yesterday,' Kiah said.

Seru smiled, but her eyes were not happy. 'Gog talked to me this morning,' she said. Her brother came in with the coffee and sandwiches and Seru began to eat. 'Gog wants to know about Zadak, and about you,' she said. 'He's going to kill us all, I think, before he goes to Mars.'

Suddenly, Rilla felt ill. 'I can't eat now!' she cried. But

Seru's brother came in with coffee and sandwiches.

she took some coffee and began to drink. 'Let's get out of here,' she said. 'Perhaps we can get a plane to Brazil and go to my family.'

'Difficult,' Seru said. 'Last night fires began in the new forest in Europe, and they're moving across Europe. The fires in Africa are burning fast. Gog began to destroy Zadak's forest in Australia yesterday.'

'Did you phone Adai?' Kiah asked.

'Adai! You never stop talking about Adai. What can he do?' Rilla said. She felt angry.

Seru looked at Rilla for a minute. 'Yes, I phoned Adai before I came here. I told him about Zadak and Bel, and about the fires. He asked about you, Kiah. He can't come down at Kisangani airport because Gog is there with a lot of his guards. Ship MARS 4 is nearly ready and Gog is watching it. He wants to leave Earth tomorrow.'

'How can Adai help us?' Rilla asked. 'He can't shoot all the guards here.'

Captain Seru finished the last sandwich. 'Let's leave that to Adai,' she said. 'We can do nothing.'

'Are you going to stay here?' Kiah asked.

'Yes,' Seru answered. 'Adai is coming to the prison after he arrives on Earth.'

'Oh yes?' Rilla said tiredly. 'But when? Gog can kill us before Adai comes.'

'No, he can't,' Seru's brother said. 'You can stay here,

in this room. Gog's guards are all afraid – afraid of the fires, afraid of the people. They aren't going to look for you here.'

6

Spaceship to the Moon

And so they waited. And waited. Rilla slept in her chair. Kiah and Seru talked quietly. Seru's brother came and went. Most of the prison guards ran away, with the prisoners. Seven or eight people – some prisoners and some guards – didn't want to run away, so they came into the room and waited, too.

Ten o'clock came, then eleven o'clock. It was very quiet. Seru walked up and down the room. Kiah sat next to Rilla. Seru's brother came into the room again.

'It's after midnight,' he said.

Just then, they heard the noise of a plane. Kiah stood up. 'Come on,' he said. 'Let's get out of the building.'

Quietly, they left the building. It was a dark, hot night. There were no guards in front of the prison, so they went to the gate and waited there. Suddenly, they saw the plane. It was a little plane, and it came down on the road in front of the prison.

Suddenly, they saw the plane.

Rilla took Kiah's hand. 'You were right,' she said. 'I'm sorry.'

Kiah smiled. He began to feel happy. 'That's all right. I understand. I know Adai very well, and you don't.'

The plane stopped and someone opened the door. Kiah ran across to the plane.

'How many can you take?' he called. 'There are twelve of us.'

'That's all right,' someone said. 'Quickly, the spaceship is waiting.'

The twelve people got into the little plane, and the plane began to move. Rilla looked at the captain of the plane. He was tall, with brown hair. He looked nice. Was this the famous Commander Adai?

'Where is the spaceship?' Kiah asked.

'At the old airport,' Adai said. 'One of the fires is moving very quickly across the new forest. It's going to arrive at the west of Kisangani before tomorrow, I think. But the old airport is OK.'

Then Commander Adai looked at Kiah and smiled warmly. 'My brother,' he said. 'My little brother, in prison 888!'

'Your brother? Commander Adai?' Rilla asked. 'But you didn't tell me that!'

Kiah smiled. 'Nobody knew,' he said. 'But now – it doesn't matter now. Everyone can know.'

The little plane came down at the old airport, south of the town.

'Let's be careful,' Adai said. 'We don't want someone to shoot us before we leave.'

The spaceship was dark. Quickly, everyone jumped down from the plane and ran across to the spaceship. Soon, the spaceship left Earth, and everyone looked down at the burning planet. They saw the dark smoke over Africa, and, here and there, through the smoke, the red, angry fires.

'The fires are destroying the forest very quickly,' Seru said.

Adai put his hand on Kiah's arm. 'I'm sorry about Zadak,' he said.

'I wanted him to wait,' Kiah said. 'I wanted him to talk to you.'

Adai's face was sad. 'He didn't want me to die,' he said quietly. 'He was a good man. And now he's dead.'

'And Gog is going to Mars,' Seru said.

'Mars? He's crazy! Mars isn't ready for people,' Adai said.

'But Gog wants to go, and so he's going,' Seru said. 'Tell us about the Moon colony. That isn't ready: you need more money.'

'No, I don't,' Adai said. 'The Moon colony is ready. I asked for more money because of Zadak. I wanted to

They saw the dark smoke over Africa.

give him money for rain. But Gog didn't listen; he wanted all Earth's money for the spaceship to Mars.'

'I don't want to leave Earth,' Rilla said sadly. She felt tired and afraid.

Adai smiled warmly at Rilla. 'Nobody wants to leave Earth,' he said. 'But under the Moon is the best home for us now. Wait and see. The Moon colony is a beautiful, wonderful country, with rivers and rain, forests and flowers, buildings – and the first town. You can visit Earth again soon, and bring more people to the Moon colony. We all want to help Earth, because it's our first home. I know that. At the same time, you *are* going to be happy under the Moon.'

Suddenly, someone cried: 'Look at the Moon!'

And through the window of the spaceship they saw the Moon before them, cold, white and beautiful; and there, under the Moon, was the Moon colony.

Back   Forward   Reload   Home   Search   Guide   Images

Universal Planet News   *16.06.2522*

EARTH BURNS

Fire is destroying our planet. First, the African forest began to burn. Then the Australian forest began to burn. Now the European forest is burning. Next, the fires are going to burn the towns. What is going to happen to our planet Earth? Earth Commander waits. What is he going to do next? What can he do? Who can help Earth and its people now? The people of Earth are waiting.

Our cameras watch Earth die.

Goodbye!

UNIVERSAL PLANET NEWS: IT'S OUT OF THIS WORLD!

GLOSSARY

AOL Artificial Ozone Layer (something only in this story)
artificial made by people
break up to break into small pieces
burn to be on fire
captain the man or woman in charge of a ship or aeroplane
colony a place where people from a different country (or planet) live
commander a man or woman in charge of many other people
crazy mad or very stupid
destroy when something is destroyed, it is dead and finished (e.g. fire burns and destroys a forest)
Earth this world; the planet we live on
fall (past tense **fell**) to go down suddenly
fire something burning
floor the part of a room that you walk on
forest a big piece of land with a lot of trees
gate a door in a fence or wall
guard a man or woman who watches for danger, or who stops prisoners from leaving
gun a thing that shoots out pieces of metal (bullets) to kill or hurt people
hole an opening in something
jump to move quickly, with both feet off the ground, from one place to another
moon the big thing that moves round the Earth and shines in the sky at night
ozone layer dangerous light from the sun is stopped by the ozone layer before it can destroy living things on Earth

planet   a large round thing in space (e.g. Earth, Mars) which moves round the sun

prison   a place where people are locked up

return   to go back

sad   not happy

satellite   a thing that people send into space; satellites move round the Earth and send back information (pictures, television, radio signals)

send (past tense **sent**)   to make someone or something go somewhere

shoot (past tense **shot**)   to send a bullet from a gun and kill or hurt something

shout   to talk very loudly

space   the place far away from the Earth, where all the planets and stars are

spaceship   something that can carry people into space

Under the Moon

ACTIVITIES

Before Reading

1 **Read the story introduction on the first page of the book, and the back cover. How much do you know now about this story? Tick one box for each sentence.**

YES NO

1 The Artificial Ozone Layer is breaking up. ☐ ☐
2 The AOL is a thousand years old. ☐ ☐
3 In the year 2522 people are living in a
   colony under the Moon. ☐ ☐
4 The forests are dying. ☐ ☐
5 There is a lot of water in the rivers. ☐ ☐
6 Kiah and Rilla are in a spaceship when
   they see the danger. ☐ ☐
7 Gog is Commander of the Moon colony. ☐ ☐
8 Gog listens to Kiah and Rilla. ☐ ☐

2 **What do you think about science-fiction stories? Choose words to finish these sentences.**

Science-fiction stories . . .
1 are usually about *the past* / *the present* / *the future*.
2 are often about living *in towns* / *in different countries* /
   on different planets.
3 *sometimes* / *always* / *never* come true.

While Reading

Read the *Universal Planet News* on page 1, and Chapter 1. Here are some untrue sentences about them. Change them into true sentences.

1 People began building the AOL on 1st January 2222.
2 Under the AOL the sun could burn the Earth.
3 In 2522 there were small holes in the AOL.
4 Two years ago, Earth Commander sent Captain Seru to a weather ship because he liked her.
5 Captain Seru wanted to talk to Gog about the AOL.
6 When Kiah and Rilla returned to Earth, they wanted to visit Adai, Commander of the Moon colony.

Read Chapter 2 and the *Universal Planet News* on page 12, and then answer these questions.

Who
1 . . . came out of his office and got on a train?
2 . . . drove the taxi in front of the train?
3 . . . began to hit Kiah?
4 . . . talked to Zadak two years ago about the AOL?
5 . . . wanted to talk to Gog about rain?
6 . . . sent Adai to the Moon colony?
7 . . . wanted more money for the Moon colony?

Read Chapter 3 and the *Universal Planet News* on page 19. Who said this, and to whom?

1 'I saw Earth Commander and talked to him about rain.'
2 'We have new numbers from the satellite.'
3 'You're going to be sorry!'
4 'Everyone comes here and wants money.'
5 'You're not going to the Moon, you're going to prison.'
6 'After the forests die, then people are going to die, too.'

Before you read Chapter 4, can you guess which two people are going to die in the chapter?

Rilla and Kiah   Gog and Bel   Zadak and Bel
Rilla and Zadak   Gog and Kiah   Zadak and Gog

Read Chapter 4 and the *Universal Planet News* on page 27. Choose the best question-word for these questions, and then answer them.

What / Where / Who
1 . . . did a guard at the prison do at midnight?
2 . . . wanted to kill Gog?
3 . . . did Kiah want Zadak to do?
4 . . . did Zadak go the next morning?
5 . . . did Zadak shoot?
6 . . . did the guards shoot?
7 . . . did it begin to rain three months ago?

Read Chapter 5. Who said this, and to whom?

1 'I'm going to destroy Australia.'
2 'One day someone is going to kill you.'
3 'You were right. Gog sent us to prison because we told him about the holes in the AOL.'
4 'You were right. Those satellite numbers were very bad.'
5 'You never stop talking about Adai. What can he do?'
6 'Adai is coming to the prison after he arrives on Earth.'

Before you read Chapter 6, can you guess what happens? Choose some of these sentences.

1 Adai returns to Earth but Gog's guards shoot him.
2 Adai finds Gog and kills him.
3 Adai takes his friends to the Moon colony.
4 Gog goes with them to the Moon colony.
5 Rilla stays on Earth and goes to her family in Brazil.
6 The Moon colony is not ready for people.
7 The Moon colony has rivers and rain, forests and flowers, and a town.
8 Adai asked for more money for the Moon colony because he wanted to give it to Zadak for rain.
9 The fires on Earth stop burning.
10 The fires on Earth are going to destroy the planet.

Now read Chapter 6 and the *Universal Planet News* on page 40. Were your guesses right?

After Reading

1 **Match the people with the sentences. Then use the sentences to write about the people. Use pronouns (*he, she, they*) and linking words (*and, and then, because*).**

Kiah and Rilla / Gog / Bel / Zadak / Adai

Example: *Bel was Gog's wife, and she liked . . .*

1 _____ was Earth Commander.
2 _____ worked on Ship OM–45.
3 _____ was Commander of Australia.
4 _Bel_ was Gog's wife.
5 _____ was Commander of the Moon colony.
6 _Bel_ liked expensive things.
7 _____ was not interested in the AOL or in planet Earth.
8 _____ talked to Gog about rain.
9 _____ went to Australia.
10 _____ returned to Earth from the Moon colony.
11 _____ saw Zadak's gun and shouted for the guards.
12 _____ talked to Zadak about the holes in the AOL.
13 _____ wanted to go to Mars.
14 _____ ran across the room to Gog.
15 _____ wanted to help his brother and his friends.
16 _____ needed rain for the new forests.

2 Here is a telephone conversation between Zadak and Adai (see page 23). The conversation is in the wrong order. Write it out in the correct order and put in the speakers' names. Zadak speaks first (number 7).

1 _____ 'Tomorrow? No, Zadak! Wait for me!'

2 _____ 'No – he doesn't want to listen. Your brother was there, too, at Earth Commander's office.'

3 _____ 'The forest is dying, because there is no rain. I talked to Earth Commander this morning.'

4 _____ 'But I don't want you to die. Earth needs you!'

5 _____ 'Yes, he is. So I'm going to kill him tomorrow.'

6 _____ 'Kiah? Why was Kiah there?'

7 _____ 'Adai? Zadak here.'

8 _____ 'He's in prison now? Gog is crazy!'

9 _____ 'But the Moon colony is ready, and I'm going to return to Earth next week.'

10 _____ 'And Earth is going to need you and the Moon colony, too. Goodbye, Adai, and good luck!'

11 _____ 'Zadak! How are you? How's the forest?'

12 _____ 'He was there to talk to Gog about the AOL – and now he's in prison 888.'

13 _____ 'Next week, next week . . . Yes, come back after Gog is dead – after I am dead too, perhaps.'

14 _____ 'What did he say? Is he going to give you money?'

15 _____ 'I can't wait for you, Adai. You need to finish the Moon colony.'

3 Find these words in the word search, and draw lines through them. The words go from left to right, and from top to bottom.

airport, burn, crazy, destroy, earth, fire, forest, guard, gun, planet, prison, satellite, shoot

S	A	T	E	L	L	I	T	E	I
M	G	G	U	N	O	I	P	N	G
E	C	R	A	Z	Y	T	L	O	L
A	E	B	U	R	N	A	A	V	A
R	F	O	R	E	S	T	N	E	I
T	T	S	H	O	O	T	E	H	R
H	F	I	R	E	I	S	T	D	P
E	A	D	G	U	A	R	D	P	O
L	P	R	I	S	O	N	A	N	R
E	T	D	E	S	T	R	O	Y	T

Now write down all the letters that don't have a line through them. (Begin with the first line and go across each line to the end.) There are twenty-eight letters, and they make a sentence of seven words.

1 What is the sentence?
2 Who said it, and to whom?
3 Where did the speaker want to go?
4 Where was Adai at that time?

4 **What happened next? Here are four different endings. Fill in the gaps with these words. (Use each word once.) Which ending or endings do you like best?**

before, changed, colony, destroyed, died, Earth, forests, live, lived, many, Mars, never, Ozone, planet, ready, returned, spaceships, towns, were

1 Gog left Earth and went to _____. The rain _____ the planet and Gog built more _____. He sent _____ to Earth and many people came to _____ on Mars.

2 Gog waited at Kisangani airport. But _____ his spaceship was _____, the fires destroyed Kisangani. Gog _____ in the fire. And so he _____ went to Mars.

3 Earth's _____ burned for months and _____ people died. Then the people on the Moon _____ began to work on the Artificial _____ Layer. After many years, they returned to _____ and began to help the _____.

4 Adai _____ on the Moon colony with Rilla, Kiah and their friends. They _____ happy there, but they never _____ to Earth because the fires _____ the planet.

5 **What did you think about this story? Complete these sentences (use as many words as you want).**

1 _____ was *right/wrong* to _____.
2 I felt sorry for _____ when _____.
3 I felt angry with _____ when _____.

51

ABOUT THE AUTHOR

Rowena Akinyemi is British, and after many years in Africa, she now lives and works in Cambridge. She has worked in English Language Teaching for twenty years, in Africa and England, and has been writing ELT fiction for ten years. She has written several other stories for the Oxford Bookworms Library, including *The Witches of Pendle* and *Remember Miranda* (both at Stage 1). She has also written books for children.

When she lived in Africa, she became interested in things like forests and the ozone layer, and she has written a book about the rainforests for the Bookworms Factfiles series, *Rainforests* (at Stage 2). The idea for her story *Under the Moon* began when her young son was worried about the future of the Earth, and asked her, 'What will happen if the holes in the ozone layer get bigger?' And that was when she thought of the idea of an Artificial Ozone Layer.

ABOUT BOOKWORMS

OXFORD BOOKWORMS LIBRARY

Classics • True Stories • Fantasy & Horror • Human Interest
Crime & Mystery • Thriller & Adventure

The OXFORD BOOKWORMS LIBRARY offers a wide range of original and adapted stories, both classic and modern, which take learners from elementary to advanced level through six carefully graded language stages:

Stage 1 (400 headwords)	Stage 4 (1400 headwords)
Stage 2 (700 headwords)	Stage 5 (1800 headwords)
Stage 3 (1000 headwords)	Stage 6 (2500 headwords)

More than fifty titles are also available on cassette, and there are many titles at Stages 1 to 4 which are specially recommended for younger learners. In addition to the introductions and activities in each Bookworm, resource material includes photocopiable test worksheets and Teacher's Handbooks, which contain advice on running a class library and using cassettes, and the answers for the activities in the books.

Several other series are linked to the OXFORD BOOKWORMS LIBRARY. They range from highly illustrated readers for young learners, to playscripts, non-fiction readers, and unsimplified texts for advanced learners.

Oxford Bookworms Starters	*Oxford Bookworms Factfiles*
Oxford Bookworms Playscripts	*Oxford Bookworms Collection*

Details of these series and a full list of all titles in the OXFORD BOOKWORMS LIBRARY can be found in the *Oxford English* catalogues. A selection of titles from the OXFORD BOOKWORMS LIBRARY can be found on the next pages.

Christmas in Prague

JOYCE HANNAM

In a house in Oxford three people are having breakfast – Carol, her husband Jan, and his father Josef. They are talking about Prague, because Carol wants them all to go there for Christmas.

Josef was born in Prague, but he left his home city when he was a young man. He is an old man now, and he would like to see Prague again before he dies. But he is afraid. He still remembers another Christmas in Prague, many long years ago – a Christmas that changed his life for ever . . .

The President's Murderer

JENNIFER BASSETT

The President is dead!

A man is running in the night. He is afraid and needs to rest. But there are people behind him – people with lights, and dogs, and guns.

A man is standing in front of a desk. His boss is very angry, and the man is tired and needs to sleep. But first he must find the other man, and bring him back – dead or alive.

Two men: the hunter and the hunted. Which will win and which will lose?

Long live the President!

Mutiny on the Bounty

TIM VICARY

It is night in the south seas near Tahiti, and the ship *HMS Bounty* has begun the long voyage home to England. But the sailors on the ship are angry men, and they have swords and guns. They pull the captain out of bed and take him up on deck. He tries to run, but a sailor holds a knife to his neck. 'Do that again, Captain Bligh, and you're a dead man!' he says.

The mutiny on the *Bounty* happened in April, 1789. This is the true story of Captain Bligh and Fletcher Christian, and the ship that never came home to England.

The Witches of Pendle

ROWENA AKINYEMI

Witches are dangerous. They can kill you with a look, or a word. They can send their friend the Devil after you in the shape of a dog or a cat. They can make a clay picture of you, then break it . . . and a few weeks later you are dead.

Today, of course, most people don't believe in witches. But in 1612 everybody was afraid of them. Young Jennet Device in Lancashire knew a lot about them because she lived with the Witches of Pendle. They were her family . . .

The Monkey's Paw

W. W. JACOBS

Retold by Diane Mowat

Outside, the night is cold and wet. Inside, the White family sits and waits. Where is their visitor?

There is a knock at the door. A man is standing outside in the dark. Their visitor has arrived.

The visitor waits. He has been in India for many years. What has he got? He has brought the hand of a small, dead animal – a monkey's paw.

Outside, in the dark, the visitor smiles and waits for the door to open.

Return to Earth

JOHN CHRISTOPHER

Retold by Susan Binder

As they walk through a park in the distant future, Harl and Ellen talk about their work and their lives. But they will never have a life together because their work as scientists is more important to them than their love. Harl plans to leave Earth, on a long and dangerous journey through space. Ellen plans to stay on Earth, to change the way the human mind works.

When Harl returns to Earth, Ellen will be long dead . . . and the world will be a very different place.